Then and Now

by Mary Lindeen

Consultant:
Adria F. Klein, PhD
California State University, San Bernardino

CAPSTONE PRESS
a capstone imprint

Wonder Readers are published by Capstone Press,
1710 Roe Crest Drive, North Mankato, Minnesota 56003.
www.capstonepub.com

Library of Congress Cataloging-in-Publication Data
Lindeen, Mary.
 Then and Now / Mary Lindeen. — 1st ed.
   p. cm. — (Wonder readers)
 Includes index.
 ISBN 978-1-4296-9616-6 (library binding)
 ISBN 978-1-4296-7972-5 (paperback)
 ISBN 978-1-62065-374-6 (ebook PDF)
 1. Social change—Juvenile literature. 2. Technological innovations—Social aspects—Juvenile literature.
 3. Innovations—Juvenile literature. I. Title.
 HM831.L566 2013
 303.48'3—dc23   2011022004

Summary: Simple text and color photos present the way inventions have changed our world in the
past and present.

Note to Parents and Teachers

The Wonder Readers: Social Studies series supports national social studies
standards. These titles use text structures that support early readers, specifically
with a close photo/text match and glossary. Each book is perfectly leveled to
support the reader at the right reading level, and the topics are of high interest.
Early readers will gain success when they are presented with a book that is of
interest to them and is written at the appropriate level.

Printed in the United States of America in North Mankato, Minnesota.
042012   006682CGF12

Table of Contents

Inventions

Everything changes. You grow and change. You look different. You have new ideas and try different things. So do other people. This is how **inventions** are born.

New inventions seem like great ideas at the time. Inventions change the way people live. People get used to the changes. Then another invention comes along, and it seems like an even better idea. This is the story of some important inventions.

See the Light

Long ago, people would light candles or gas lamps when it got dark. It still was not easy to see at night.

Then a scientist invented the **lightbulb**. It made brighter light than a flame. It was easier for people to work, read, and play at night. The lightbulb changed people's lives.

Talk to Me

Long ago, people had to write letters if they wanted to "talk" to someone who lived far away. Then Alexander Graham Bell invented the telephone in 1876.

For many years, telephones had to be attached to wires in the walls. Then people invented **cell phones**. Now we can use telephones wherever we go!

Horse Power

Long ago, people traveled from place to place on horses. They either rode on a horse's back or in a cart or wagon pulled by a horse. It could take several days to get from one town to another.

Then people invented motorized vehicles. The vehicles could go farther and faster than horses. It was quicker and easier to go from place to place. Travel and work got even easier as more vehicles were invented.

Let's Eat

Long ago, people cooked their food over fires. Then people invented the wood stove. The wood stove made cooking safer and easier. Soon the gas stove was invented. Cooking became even easier with a gas stove.

Then came the electric stove, which made cooking safer. Now people use **microwave ovens**. Food cooks in just a few minutes.

Say Cheese!

Long ago, the only way to get a
picture of someone was to draw
or paint it. In the 1800s, people
invented cameras. Cameras were
pretty big and tricky to use. Only a
few people knew how to use them.

Now we use **digital** cameras. They are easy to use and can take many different kinds of pictures. Today most people own a camera. There are even tiny cameras built into cell phones and computers.

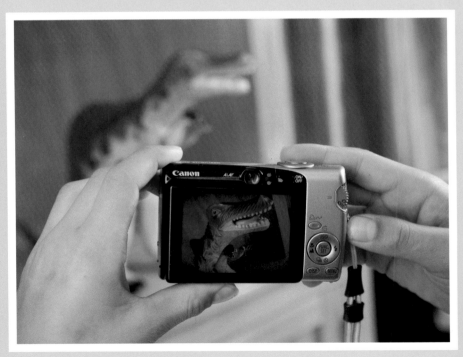

Walk or Ride?

Long ago, people had to walk or ride a horse when they wanted to travel a short distance. Then people invented bicycles. The first bicycle had a very big front wheel and a wooden seat.

Now bicycles are much safer and more comfortable to ride. They have padded seats and brakes. They come in many styles and colors. They go fast too. Thank goodness someone invented helmets!

Glossary

cell phone   a wireless telephone that uses radio waves to send and receive calls

digital   recording text, images, or sound in a format that can be used on a computer

invention   a new device or machine that is made based on an idea someone has

lightbulb   a glass bulb with a filament inside that glows and gives off light when electricity flows through it

microwave oven   a small electric oven that uses radio waves to cook food quickly

Now Try This!

Imagine what life will be like 100 years from now. How will we travel? What will our homes look like? What will we do for fun? Draw or write your ideas about life in the future. Compare life now to the life you imagine for the future. What do you think will change? What do you think will stay the same? Why do you think so?

Internet Sites

FactHound offers a safe, fun way to find Internet sites related to this book. All of the sites on FactHound have been researched by our staff.

Here's all you do:

Visit *www.facthound.com*

Type in this code: 9781429696166

 Check out projects, games and lots more at
www.capstonekids.com

Index

Editorial Credits
Maryellen Gregoire, project director; Mary Lindeen, consulting editor; Gene Bentdahl, designer; Sarah Schuette, editor; Wanda Winch, media researcher; Eric Manske, production specialist

Photo Credits
Photos by Capstone Studio: Karon Dubke except: Shutterstock: Dja65, 14, Elzbieta Sekowska, 10, Inc, 12, KJBevan, 6, Nicolas, McComber, 8, Toenne, 16

Word Count: **448**   Guided Reading Level: K   Early Intervention Level: **17**